THE DENVER BRONCOS

BY THOMAS K. ADAMSON

EPIC

BELLWETHER MEDIA ★ MINNEAPOLIS, MN

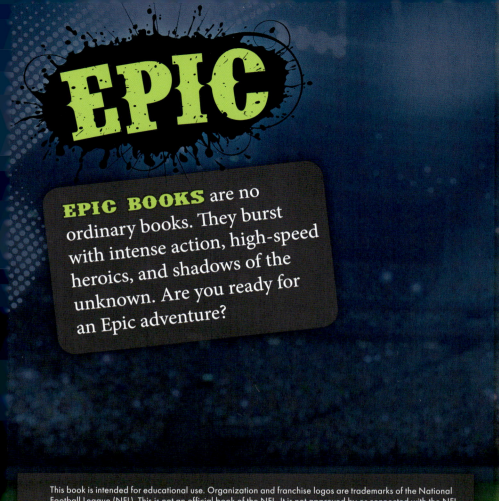

EPIC

EPIC BOOKS are no ordinary books. They burst with intense action, high-speed heroics, and shadows of the unknown. Are you ready for an Epic adventure?

This book is intended for educational use. Organization and franchise logos are trademarks of the National Football League (NFL). This is not an official book of the NFL. It is not approved by or connected with the NFL.

This edition first published in 2024 by Bellwether Media, Inc.

No part of this publication may be reproduced in whole or in part without written permission of the publisher. For information regarding permission, write to Bellwether Media, Inc., Attention: Permissions Department, 6012 Blue Circle Drive, Minnetonka, MN 55343.

Library of Congress Cataloging-in-Publication Data

Names: Adamson, Thomas K., 1970- author.
Title: The Denver Broncos / by Thomas K. Adamson.
Description: Minneapolis, MN : Bellwether Media, Inc. 2024. | Series: Epic: NFL team profiles | Includes bibliographical references and index. | Audience: Ages 7-12 | Audience: Grades 2-3 | Summary: "Engaging images accompany information about the Denver Broncos. The combination of high-interest subject matter and light text is intended for students in grades 2 through 7"-- Provided by publisher.
Identifiers: LCCN 2023021279 (print) | LCCN 2023021280 (ebook) | ISBN 9798886874754 (library binding) | ISBN 9798886876635 (ebook)
Subjects: LCSH: Denver Broncos (Football team)--Juvenile literature. | Football teams--Colorado--Denver--Juvenile literature.
Classification: LCC GV956.D37 A33 2024 (print) | LCC GV956.D37 (ebook) | DDC 796.332/640978883--dc23/eng/20230515
LC record available at https://lccn.loc.gov/2023021279
LC ebook record available at https://lccn.loc.gov/2023021280

Text copyright © 2024 by Bellwether Media, Inc. EPIC and associated logos are trademarks and/or registered trademarks of Bellwether Media, Inc.

Editor: Elizabeth Neuenfeldt   Designer: Gabriel Hilger

Printed in the United States of America, North Mankato, MN.

TABLE OF CONTENTS

SUPER BOWL STRIP SACK	4
THE HISTORY OF THE BRONCOS	6
THE BRONCOS TODAY	14
GAME DAY!	16
DENVER BRONCOS FACTS	20
GLOSSARY	22
TO LEARN MORE	23
INDEX	24

SUPER BOWL STRIP SACK

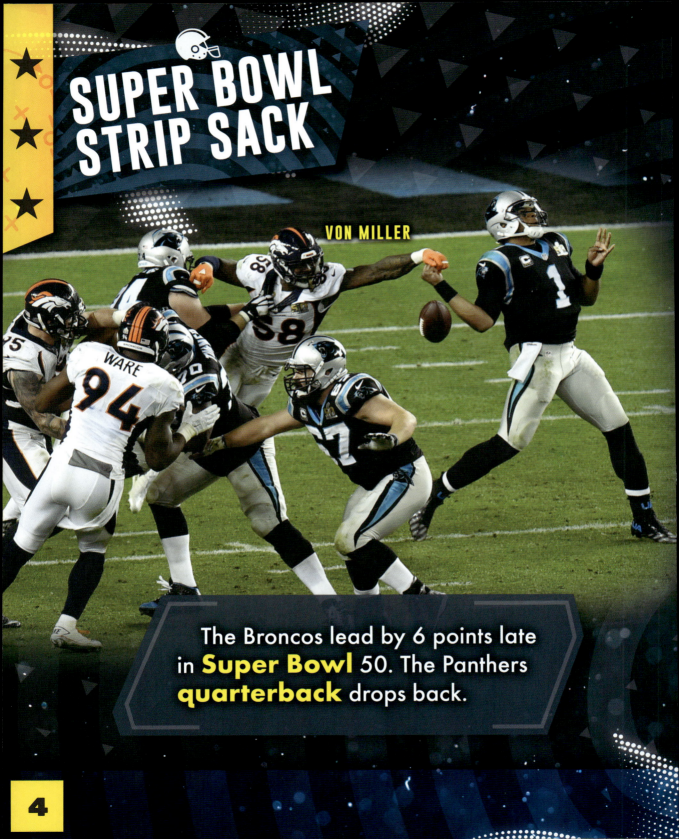

VON MILLER

The Broncos lead by 6 points late in **Super Bowl** 50. The Panthers **quarterback** drops back.

Broncos **linebacker** Von Miller slaps the ball as the quarterback throws. Miller gets the **strip sack**! His play helps the Broncos win the game!

TWICE AS NICE

Von Miller had two strip sacks in the game!

THE HISTORY OF THE BRONCOS

The Broncos began in Denver, Colorado. In 1960, they joined the American Football League (AFL). In 1970, they joined National Football League (NFL).

In 1978, the team reached Super Bowl 12. But they lost to the Dallas Cowboys.

SUPER BOWL 12

OUT WITH THE OLD

The team's first uniform colors were mustard and brown. They changed to orange and blue in 1962.

DENVER, COLORADO

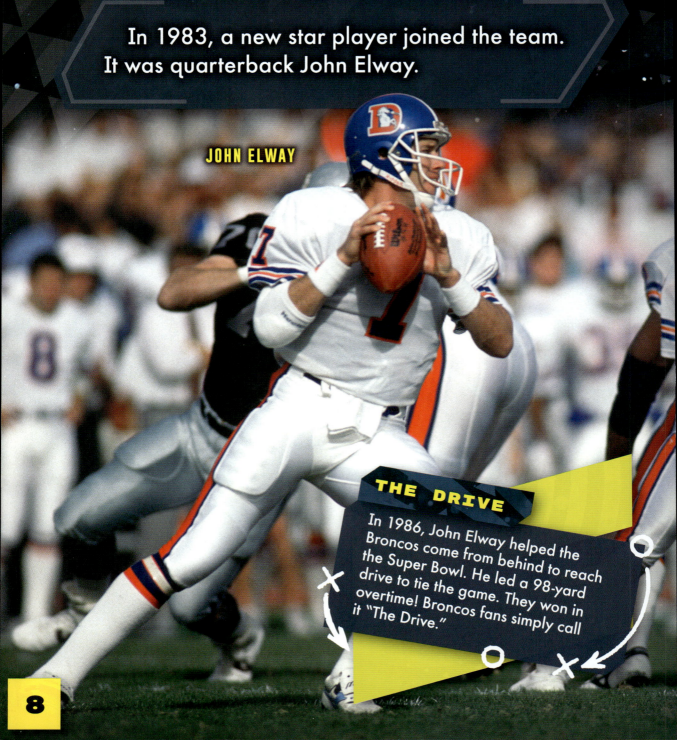

In 1983, a new star player joined the team. It was quarterback John Elway.

JOHN ELWAY

THE DRIVE

In 1986, John Elway helped the Broncos come from behind to reach the Super Bowl. He led a 98-yard drive to tie the game. They won in overtime! Broncos fans simply call it "The Drive."

8

SUPER BOWL 24

He led the team to three Super Bowls in the 1980s. But they could not win the big game.

In 1998, Elway helped the team reach Super Bowl 32. They finally won! Elway also helped the team win Super Bowl 33!

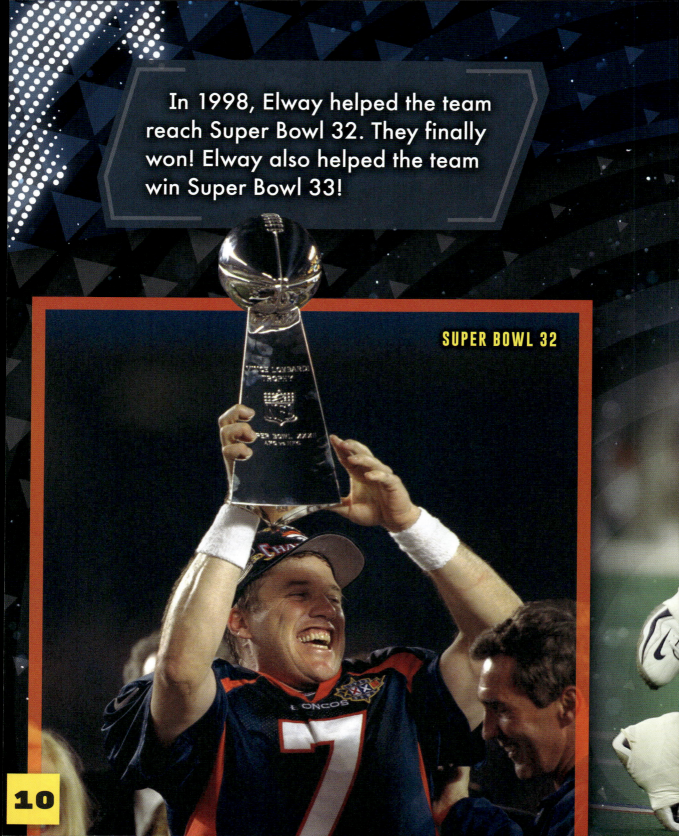

SUPER BOWL 32

The Broncos did well in the 2000s. But they could not reach the Super Bowl.

2005 BRONCOS GAME

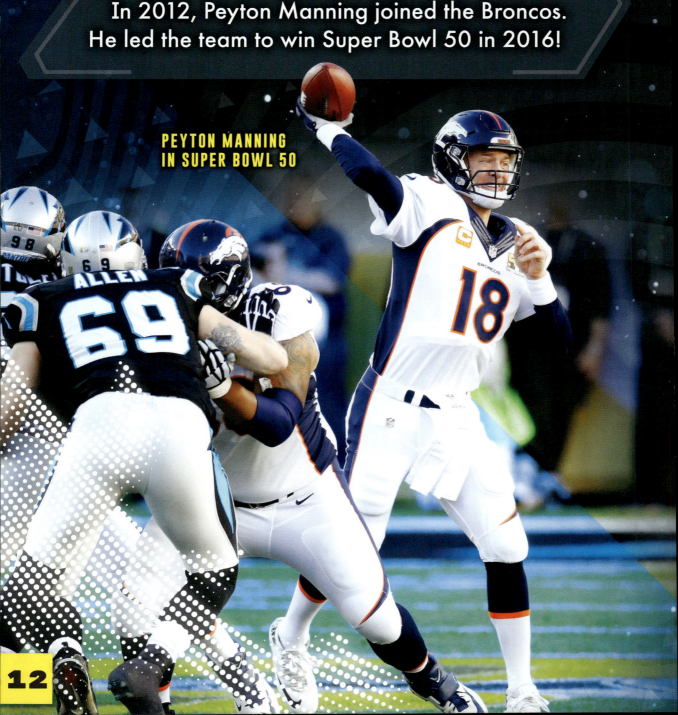

In 2012, Peyton Manning joined the Broncos. He led the team to win Super Bowl 50 in 2016!

PEYTON MANNING IN SUPER BOWL 50

The Broncos did not reach the **playoffs** for the next seven seasons. They hope to return soon.

TROPHY CASE

AFC WEST championships
15

PLAYOFF appearances
22

AFC championships
8

SUPER BOWL championships
3

THE BRONCOS TODAY

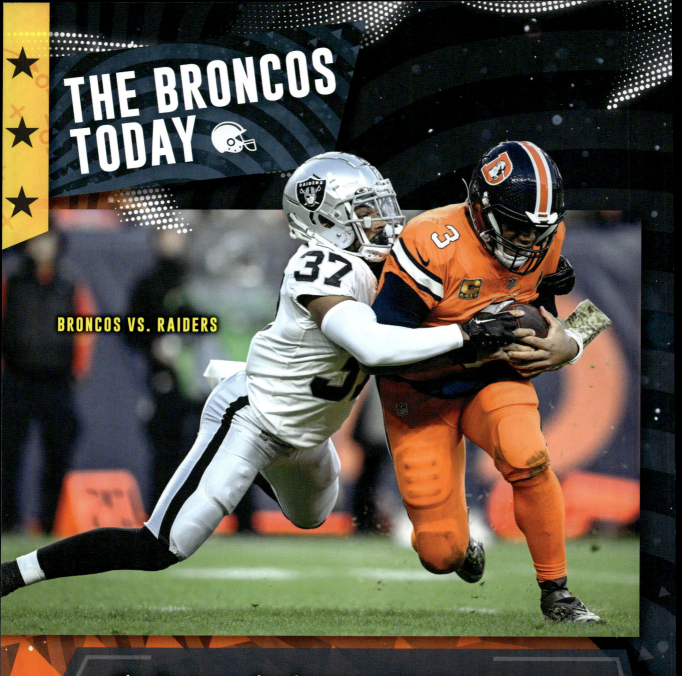

BRONCOS VS. RAIDERS

The Broncos play home games at Empower Field at Mile High **Stadium** in Denver, Colorado. It is 5,280 feet (1,609 meters), or one mile, above **sea level**!

The Broncos are part of the AFC West **division**. Their biggest **rival** is the Las Vegas Raiders.

LOCATION

COLORADO

EMPOWER FIELD AT MILE HIGH STADIUM
Denver, Colorado

GAME DAY!

The Broncos **mascot** is named Miles. He pumps up fans at home games!
 The team also has a live mascot. It is a horse named Thunder. It runs along the field when the Broncos score!

THUNDER

Broncos fans wear orange and navy blue to support their team.

They have a loud **tradition**. It happens after an opponent throws an **incomplete** pass. Fans yell that the pass is "IN-COM-PLETE!" Fans love to cheer for the Broncos!

★ FAMOUS PLAYERS ★

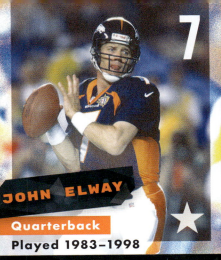

7

JOHN ELWAY

Quarterback
Played 1983–1998

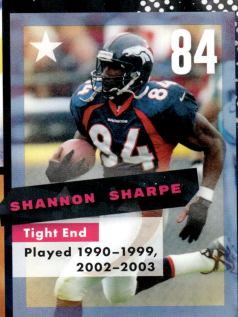

84

SHANNON SHARPE

Tight End
Played 1990–1999, 2002–2003

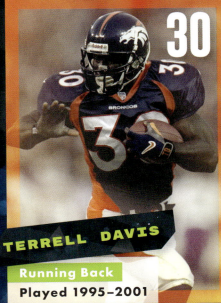

30

TERRELL DAVIS

Running Back
Played 1995–2001

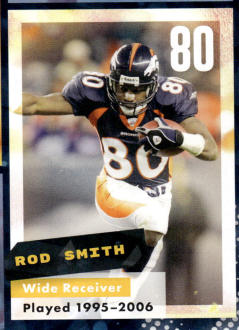

80

ROD SMITH

Wide Receiver
Played 1995–2006

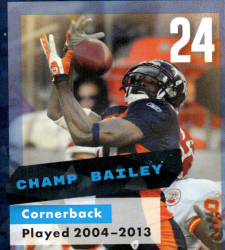

24

CHAMP BAILEY

Cornerback
Played 2004–2013

DENVER BRONCOS FACTS

LOGO

JOINED THE NFL | 1970
(AFL 1960–1969)

MASCOT

MILES

NICKNAME | None

CONFERENCE
American Football Conference (AFC)

COLORS

DIVISION | AFC West

 Kansas City Chiefs

 Las Vegas Raiders

Los Angeles Chargers

 STADIUM

★ EMPOWER FIELD AT MILE HIGH STADIUM ★

opened August 11, 2001

holds **76,125** people

20

⏰ TIMELINE

1960 — The Broncos play their first season

1978 — The Broncos play in Super Bowl 12

1983 — John Elway joins the team

1998 — The Broncos win Super Bowl 32

2016 — The Broncos win Super Bowl 50

★ RECORDS ★

All-Time Passing Leader

John Elway
51,475 yards

All-Time Rushing Leader

Terrell Davis
7,607 yards

All-Time Receiving Leader

Rod Smith
11,389 yards

Single-Season Passing Touchdowns Leader

Peyton Manning
55 touchdowns in 2013

21

GLOSSARY

division—a group of NFL teams from the same area that often play against each other; there are eight divisions in the NFL.

incomplete—not caught by anyone

linebacker—a player whose main job is to tackle opposing players

mascot—an animal or symbol that represents a sports team

playoffs—games played after the regular NFL season is over; playoff games determine which teams play in the championship game.

quarterback—a player whose main job is to throw and hand off the ball

rival—a long-standing opponent

sea level—the height of the sea's surface

stadium—an arena where sports are played

strip sack—a quarterback sack that results in the opposing player dropping the ball

Super Bowl—the annual championship game of the NFL

tradition—a special way people celebrate or honor something

TO LEARN MORE

AT THE LIBRARY

Abdo, Kenny. *Denver Broncos*. Minneapolis, Minn.: Abdo Zoom, 2022.

Leed, Percy. *Peyton Manning: Most Valuable Quarterback*. Minneapolis, Minn.: Lerner Publications, 2022.

Whiting, Jim. *The Story of the Denver Broncos*. Mankato, Minn.: Creative Education, 2020.

ON THE WEB

FACTSURFER

Factsurfer.com gives you a safe, fun way to find more information.

1. Go to www.factsurfer.com.

2. Enter "Denver Broncos" into the search box and click 🔍.

3. Select your book cover to see a list of related content.

INDEX

AFC West, 15, 20
American Football League (AFL), 6, 20
colors, 7, 18, 20
Denver, Colorado, 6, 7, 14, 15
Denver Broncos facts, 20–21
Elway, John, 8, 9, 10
Empower Field at Mile High Stadium, 14, 15, 20
famous players, 19
fans, 8, 16, 18
history, 4, 5, 6, 7, 8, 9, 10, 11, 12, 13

Manning, Peyton, 12
mascot, 16, 17, 20
Miller, Von, 4, 5
National Football League (NFL), 6, 20
playoffs, 13
positions, 4, 5, 8
records, 21
rival, 15
Super Bowl, 4, 5, 6, 8, 9, 10, 11, 12
timeline, 21
trophy case, 13

The images in this book are reproduced through the courtesy of: Paul Abell/ AP Images, cover; Chris Rubino, cover (stadium), p. 15 (Empower Field at Mile High Stadium); Icon Sportswire/ Contributor/ Getty, pp. 3, 4, 23; Patrick Smith/ Staff/ Getty, p. 5; Focus On Sport/ Contributor/ Getty, pp. 6, 8, 9, 19 (John Elway), 21 (1983, 1998); f11photo, pp. 6-7; Sporting News Archive/ Contributor/ Getty, p. 10; Al Bello/ Staff/ Getty, pp. 10-11, 12; AAron Ontiveroz/MediaNewsGroup/The Denver Post via Getty Images/ Contributor/ Getty Images, p. 14; NFL/ Wikipedia, pp. 15 (Denver Broncos logo), 20 (Broncos logo, Chiefs logo, Raiders logo, Chargers logo, AFC Logo); Justin Edmonds/ Stringer/ Getty, pp. 16, 16-17; Rob Tringali/ Contributor/ Getty, pp. 18-19; Peter Read Miller/ AP Images, p. 19 (Shannon Sharpe); Brian Bahr/ Staff/ Getty, pp. 19 (Terrell Davis, Rod Smith), 21 (Terrell Davis, Rod Smith); Steve Dykes/ Stringer/ Getty, p. 19 (Champ Bailey); Jamie Schwaberow/ Contributor/ Getty, p. 20 (mascot); Leeweh, p. 20 (stadium); Martin Mills/ Contributor/ Getty, p. 21 (1960); Nate Fine/ Contributor/ Getty, p. 21 (1978); Ezra Shaw/ Staff/ Getty, p. 21 (2016); Al Pereira/ Contributor/ Getty, p. 21 (John Elway); Doug Pensinger/ Staff/ Getty, p. 21 (Peyton Manning).